HOW TO TELL A STORY AND OTHERS

by

Mark Twain

Published by Left of Brain Books

Copyright © 2023 Left of Brain Books

ISBN 978-1-397-66752-6

First Edition

PUBLISHER'S PREFACE

About the Book

"How to Tell a Story and Other Essays is a series of essays by Mark Twain. In them he describes his own writing style, attacks the idiocy of a fellow author, defends the virtue of a dead woman, and tries to protect ordinary citizens from insults by railroad conductors."

(Quote from wikipedia.org)

About the Author

Mark Twain (1835 - 1910)

"Samuel Langhorne Clemens... better known by the pen name Mark Twain, was an American humorist, satirist, lecturer and writer. Twain is most noted for his novels Adventures of Huckleberry Finn, which has since been called the Great American Novel, and The Adventures of Tom Sawyer. He is also known for his quotations. During his lifetime, Clemens became a friend to presidents, artists, leading industrialists and European royalty.

Clemens enjoyed immense public popularity, and his keen wit and incisive satire earned him praise from both critics and peers. American author William Faulkner called Twain 'the father of American literature.'"

(Quote from wikipedia.org)

CONTENTS

PUBLISHER'S PREFACE

HOW TO TELL A STORY 1

    THE WOUNDED SOLDIER 3

    THE GOLDEN ARM 7

MENTAL TELEGRAPHY AGAIN 9

THE INVALID'S STORY 17

HOW TO TELL A STORY

The Humorous Story an American Development.--Its Difference from Comic and Witty Stories

I do not claim that I can tell a story as it ought to be told. I only claim to know how a story ought to be told, for I have been almost daily in the company of the most expert story-tellers for many years.

There are several kinds of stories, but only one difficult kind-- the humorous. I will talk mainly about that one. The humorous story is American, the comic story is English, the witty story is French. The humorous story depends for its effect upon the manner of the telling; the comic story and the witty story upon the matter.

The humorous story may be spun out to great length, and may wander around as much as it pleases, and arrive nowhere in particular; but the comic and witty stories must be brief and end with a point. The humorous story bubbles gently along, the others burst.

The humorous story is strictly a work of art--high and delicate art--and only an artist can tell it; but no art is necessary in telling the comic and the witty story; anybody can do it. The art of telling a humorous story--understand, I mean by word of mouth, not print--was created in America, and has remained at home.

The humorous story is told gravely; the teller does his best to conceal the fact that he even dimly suspects that there is anything funny about it; but the teller of the comic story tells you beforehand that it is one of the funniest things he has ever heard, then tells it with eager delight, and is the first person to laugh when he gets through. And sometimes, if he has had good success, he is so glad and happy that he will repeat the "nub" of it and glance around from face to face, collecting applause, and then repeat it again. It is a pathetic thing to see.

Very often, of course, the rambling and disjointed humorous story finishes with a nub, point, snapper, or whatever you like to call it. Then the listener must be alert, for in many cases the teller will divert attention from that nub by dropping it in a carefully casual and indifferent way, with the pretence that he does not know it is a nub.

Artemus Ward used that trick a good deal; then when the belated audience presently caught the joke he would look up with innocent surprise, as if wondering what they had found to laugh at. Dan Setchell used it before him, Nye and Riley and others use it to-day.

But the teller of the comic story does not slur the nub; he shouts it at you--every time. And when he prints it, in England, France, Germany, and Italy, he italicizes it, puts some whooping exclamation-points after it, and sometimes explains it in a parenthesis. All of which is very depressing, and makes one want to renounce joking and lead a better life.

Let me set down an instance of the comic method, using an anecdote which has been popular all over the world for twelve or fifteen hundred years. The teller tells it in this way:

THE WOUNDED SOLDIER

IN the course of a certain battle a soldier whose leg had been shot off appealed to another soldier who was hurrying by to carry him to the rear, informing him at the same time of the loss which he had sustained; whereupon the generous son of Mars, shouldering the unfortunate, proceeded to carry out his desire. The bullets and cannon-balls were flying in all directions, and presently one of the latter took the wounded man's head off-- without, however, his deliverer being aware of it. In no-long time he was hailed by an officer, who said:

"Where are you going with that carcass?"

"To the rear, sir--he's lost his leg!"

"His leg, forsooth?" responded the astonished officer; "you mean his head, you booby."

Whereupon the soldier dispossessed himself of his burden, and stood looking down upon it in great perplexity. At length he said:

"It is true, slr, just as you have said." Then after a pause he added, "But he TOLD me IT WAS HIS LEG! ! ! ! !"

Here the narrator bursts into explosion after explosion of thunderous horse-laughter, repeating that nub from time to time through his gaspings and shriekings and suffocatings.

It takes only a minute and a half to tell that in its comic-story form; and isn't worth the telling, after all. Put into the humorous-story form it takes ten minutes, and is about the funniest thing I have ever listened to--as James Whitcomb Riley tells it.

He tells it in the character of a dull-witted old farmer who has just heard it for the first time, thinks it is unspeakably funny, and is trying to repeat it to a neighbor. But he can't remember it; so he gets all mixed up and wanders helplessly round and round, putting in tedious details that don't belong in the tale and only retard it; taking them out conscientiously and putting in others that are just as useless; making minor mistakes now and then and stopping to correct them and explain how he came to make them; remembering things which he forgot to put in in their proper place and going back to put them in there; stopping his narrative a good while in order to try to recall the name of the soldier that was hurt, and finally remembering that the soldier's name was not mentioned, and remarking placidly that the name is of no real importance, anyway--better, of course, if one knew it, but not essential, after all-- and so on, and so on, and so on.

The teller is innocent and happy and pleased with himself, and has to stop every little while to hold himself in and keep from laughing outright; and does hold in, but his body quakes in a jelly-like way with interior chuckles; and at the end of the ten minutes the audience have laughed until they are exhausted, and the tears are running down their faces.

The simplicity and innocence and sincerity and unconsciousness of the old farmer are perfectly simulated, and the result is a performance which is thoroughly charming and delicious. This is art and fine and beautiful, and only a master can compass it; but a machine could tell the other story.

To string incongruities and absurdities together in a wandering and sometimes purposeless way, and seem innocently unaware that they are absurdities, is the basis of the American art, if my position is correct. Another feature is the slurring of the point. A third is the dropping of a studied remark apparently without knowing it, as if one were thinking aloud. The fourth and last is the pause.

Artemus Ward dealt in numbers three and four a good deal. He would begin to tell with great animation something which he seemed to think was wonderful; then lose confidence, and after an apparently absent-minded pause add an incongruous remark in a soliloquizing way; and that was the remark intended to explode the mine--and it did.

For instance, he would say eagerly, excitedly, "I once knew a man in New Zealand who hadn't a tooth in his head"--here his animation would die out; a silent, reflective pause would follow, then he would say dreamily, and as if to himself, "and yet that man could beat a drum better than any man I ever saw."

The pause is an exceedingly important feature in any kind of story, and a frequently recurring feature, too. It is a dainty thing, and delicate, and also uncertain and treacherous; for it must be exactly the right length--no more and no less--or it fails of its purpose and makes trouble. If the pause is too short the impressive point is passed, and [and if too long] the audience have had time to divine that a surprise is intended--and then you can't surprise them, of course.

On the platform I used to tell a negro ghost story that had a pause in front of the snapper on the end, and that pause was the most important thing in the whole story. If I got it the right length precisely, I could spring the finishing ejaculation with effect enough to make some impressible girl deliver a startled little yelp and jump out of her seat --and that was what I was after. This story was called "The Golden Arm," and was told in this fashion. You can practise with it yourself--and mind you look out for the pause and get it right.

THE GOLDEN ARM

ONCE 'pon a time dey wuz a monsus mean man, en he live 'way out in de prairie all 'lone by hisself, 'cep'n he had a wife. En bimeby she died, en he tuck en toted her way out dah in de prairie en buried her. Well, she had a golden arm--all solid gold, fum de shoulder down. He wuz pow'ful mean--pow'ful; en dat night he couldn't sleep, Gaze he want dat golden arm so bad.

When it come midnight he couldn't stan' it no mo'; so he git up, he did, en tuck his lantern en shoved out thoo de storm en dug her up en got de golden arm; en he bent his head down 'gin de win', en plowed en plowed en plowed thoo de snow. Den all on a sudden he stop (make a considerable pause here, and look startled, and take a listening attitude) en say: "My LAN', what's dat!"

En he listen--en listen--en de win' say (set your teeth together and imitate the wailing and wheezing singsong of the wind), "Bzzz-z-zzz"--- en den, way back yonder whah de grave is, he hear a voice! he hear a voice all mix' up in de win' can't hardly tell 'em 'part--" Bzzz-zzz-- W-h-o--g-o-t--m-y--g-o-l-d-e-n arm? --zzz--zzz-- W-h-o g-o-t m-y g-o-l- d-e-n arm!" (You must begin to shiver violently now.)

En he begin to shiver en shake, en say, "Oh, my! OH, my lan'! "en de win' blow de lantern out, en de snow en sleet blow in his face en mos' choke him, en he start a-plowin' knee-deep towards home mos' dead, he so sk'yerd--en pooty soon he hear de voice agin, en (pause) it 'us comin' after him! "Bzzz--zzz--zzz--W-h-o--g-o-t m-y--g-o-l-d-e-n--arm?"

When he git to de pasture he hear it agin closter now, en a-comin'!-- a-comin' back dah in de dark en de storm--(repeat the wind and the voice). When he git to de house he rush up-stairs en jump in de bed en kiver up, head and years, en lay dah shiverin' en shakin'--en den way out dah he hear it agin!--en a-comin'! En bimeby he hear (pause--awed, listening attitude)--pat--pat--pat--hit's acomin' up-stairs! Den he hear de latch, en he know it's in de room!

Den pooty soon he know it's a-stannin' by de bed! (Pause.) Den--he know it's a-bendin' down over him--en he cain't skasely git his breath! Den-- den--he seem to feel someth' n c-o-l-d, right down 'most agin his head! (Pause.)

Den de voice say, right at his year--"W-h-o g-o-t--m-y--g-o-l-d-e-n arm?" (You must wail it out very plaintively and accusingly; then you stare steadily and impressively into the face of the farthest-gone auditor--a girl, preferably--and let that awe-inspiring pause begin to build itself in the deep hush. When it has reached exactly the right length, jump suddenly at that girl and yell, "You've got it!")

If you've got the pause right, she'll fetch a dear little yelp and spring right out of her shoes. But you must get the pause right; and you will find it the most troublesome and aggravating and uncertain thing you ever undertook.

MENTAL TELEGRAPHY AGAIN

I have three or four curious incidents to tell about. They seem to come under the head of what I named "Mental Telegraphy" in a paper written seventeen years ago, and published long afterwards.--[The paper entitled "Mental Telegraphy," which originally appeared in Harper's Magazine for December, 1893, is included in the volume entitled The American Claimant and Other Stories and Sketches.]

Several years ago I made a campaign on the platform with Mr. George W. Cable. In Montreal we were honored with a reception. It began at two in the afternoon in a long drawing-room in the Windsor Hotel. Mr. Cable and I stood at one end of this room, and the ladies and gentlemen entered it at the other end, crossed it at that end, then came up the long left-hand side, shook hands with us, said a word or two, and passed on, in the usual way. My sight is of the telescopic sort, and I presently recognized a familiar face among the throng of strangers drifting in at the distant door, and I said to myself, with surprise and high gratification, "That is Mrs. R.; I had forgotten that she was a Canadian." She had been a great friend of mine in Carson City, Nevada, in the early days. I had not seen her or heard of her for twenty years; I had not been thinking about her; there was nothing to suggest her to me, nothing to bring her to my mind; in fact, to me she had long ago ceased to exist, and had disappeared from my consciousness. But I knew her instantly; and I saw her so clearly that I was able to note some of the particulars of her dress, and did note them, and they remained in my mind. I was impatient for her to come. In the midst of the hand- shakings I snatched glimpses of her and noted her progress with the slow-moving file across the end of the room; then I saw her start up the side, and this gave me a full front view of her face. I saw her last when she was within twenty-five feet of me. For an hour I kept thinking she must still be in the room somewhere and would come at last, but I was disappointed.

When I arrived in the lecture-hall that evening some one said: "Come into the waiting-room; there's a friend of yours there who wants to see you. You'll not be introduced--you are to do the recognizing without help if you can."

I said to myself: "It is Mrs. R.; I shan't have any trouble."

There were perhaps ten ladies present, all seated. In the midst of them was Mrs. R., as I had expected. She was dressed exactly as she was when I had seen her in the afternoon. I went forward and shook hands with her and called her by name, and said:

"I knew you the moment you appeared at the reception this afternoon." She looked surprised, and said: "But I was not at the reception. I have just arrived from Quebec, and have not been in town an hour."

It was my turn to be surprised now. I said: "I can't help it. I give you my word of honor that it is as I say. I saw you at the reception, and you were dressed precisely as you are now. When they told me a moment ago that I should find a friend in this room, your image rose before me, dress and all, just as I had seen you at the reception."

Those are the facts. She was not at the reception at all, or anywhere near it; but I saw her there nevertheless, and most clearly and unmistakably. To that I could make oath. How is one to explain this? I was not thinking of her at the time; had not thought of her for years. But she had been thinking of me, no doubt; did her thoughts flit through leagues of air to me, and bring with it that clear and pleasant vision of herself? I think so. That was and remains my sole experience in the matter of apparitions--I mean apparitions that come when one is (ostensibly) awake. I could have been asleep for a moment; the apparition could have been the creature of a dream. Still, that is nothing to the point; the feature of interest is the happening of the thing just at that time, instead of at an earlier or later time, which is argument that its origin lay in thought-transference.

My next incident will be set aside by most persons as being merely a "coincidence," I suppose. Years ago I used to think sometimes of making a lecturing trip through the antipodes and the borders of the Orient, but always gave up the idea, partly because of the great length of the journey and partly because my wife could not well manage to go with me. Towards the end of last January that idea, after an interval of years, came suddenly into my head again--forcefully, too, and without any apparent reason. Whence came it? What suggested it? I will touch upon that presently.

I was at that time where I am now--in Paris. I wrote at once to Henry M. Stanley (London), and asked him some questions about his Australian lecture tour, and inquired who had conducted him and what were the terms. After a day or two his answer came. It began:

"The lecture agent for Australia and New Zealand is par excellence Mr. R. S. Smythe, of Melbourne."

He added his itinerary, terms, sea expenses, and some other matters, and advised me to write Mr. Smythe, which I did--February 3d. I began my letter by saying in substance that while he did not know me personally we had a mutual friend in Stanley, and that would answer for an introduction. Then I proposed my trip, and asked if he would give me the same terms which he had given Stanley.

I mailed my letter to Mr. Smythe February 6th, and three days later I got a letter from the selfsame Smythe, dated Melbourne, December 17th. I would as soon have expected to get a letter from the late George Washington. The letter began somewhat as mine to him had begun--with a self-introduction:

"DEAR MR. CLEMENS,--It is so long since Archibald Forbes and I spent that pleasant afternoon in your comfortable house at Hartford that you have probably quite forgotten the occasion."

In the course of his letter this occurs:

"I am willing to give you" [here be named the terms which he had given Stanley] "for an antipodean tour to last, say, three months."

Here was the single essential detail of my letter answered three days after I had mailed my inquiry. I might have saved myself the trouble and the postage--and a few years ago I would have done that very thing, for I would have argued that my sudden and strong impulse to write and ask some questions of a stranger on the under side of the globe meant that the impulse came from that stranger, and that he would answer my questions of his own motion if I would let him alone.

Mr. Smythe's letter probably passed under my nose on its way to lose three weeks traveling to America and back, and gave me a whiff of its contents as it went along. Letters often act like that. Instead of the thought coming to you in an instant from

Australia, the (apparently) unsentient letter imparts it to you as it glides invisibly past your elbow in the mail-bag.

Next incident. In the following month--March--I was in America. I spent a Sunday at Irvington-on-the-Hudson with Mr. John Brisben Walker, of the Cosmopolitan magazine. We came into New York next morning, and went to the Century Club for luncheon. He said some praiseful things about the character of the club and the orderly serenity and pleasantness of its quarters, and asked if I had never tried to acquire membership in it. I said I had not, and that New York clubs were a continuous expense to the country members without being of frequent use or benefit to them.

"And now I've got an idea!" said I. "There's the Lotos--the first New York club I was ever a member of--my very earliest love in that line. I have been a member of it for considerably more than twenty years, yet have seldom had a chance to look in and see the boys. They turn gray and grow old while I am not watching. And my dues go on. I am going to Hartford this afternoon for a day or two, but as soon as I get back I will go to John Elderkin very privately and say: 'Remember the veteran and confer distinction upon him, for the sake of old times. Make me an honorary member and abolish the tax. If you haven't any such thing as honorary membership, all the better--create it for my honor and glory.' That would be a great thing; I will go to John Elderkin as soon as I get back from Hartford."

I took the last express that afternoon, first telegraphing Mr. F. G. Whitmore to come and see me next day. When he came he asked: "Did you get a letter from Mr. John Elderkin, secretary of the Lotos Club, before you left New York?"

"Then it just missed you. If I had known you were coming I would have kept it. It is beautiful, and will make you proud. The Board of Directors, by unanimous vote, have made you a life member, and squelched those dues; and, you are to be on hand and receive your distinction on the night of the 30th, which is the twenty-fifth anniversary of the founding of the club, and it will not surprise me if they have some great times there."

What put the honorary membership in my head that day in the Century Club? for I had never thought of it before. I don't know what brought the thought to me at that particular time instead of earlier, but I am well satisfied that it originated with the Board of Directors, and had been on its way to my brain through the air ever since the moment that saw their vote recorded.

Another incident. I was in Hartford two or three days as a guest of the Rev. Joseph H. Twichell. I have held the rank of Honorary Uncle to his children for a quarter of a century, and I went out with him in the trolley-car to visit one of my nieces, who is at Miss Porter's famous school in Farmington. The distance is eight or nine miles. On the way, talking, I illustrated something with an anecdote. This is the anecdote:

Two years and a half ago I and the family arrived at Milan on our way to Rome, and stopped at the Continental. After dinner I went below and took a seat in the stone-paved court, where the customary lemon-trees stand in the customary tubs, and said to myself, "Now this is comfort, comfort and repose, and nobody to disturb it; I do not know anybody in Milan."

Then a young gentleman stepped up and shook hands, which damaged my theory. He said, in substance:

"You won't remember me, Mr. Clemens, but I remember you very well. I was a cadet at West Point when you and Rev. Joseph

H. Twichell came there some years ago and talked to us on a Hundredth Night. I am a lieutenant in the regular army now, and my name is H. I am in Europe, all alone, for a modest little tour; my regiment is in Arizona."

We became friendly and sociable, and in the course of the talk he told me of an adventure which had befallen him--about to this effect:

"I was at Bellagio, stopping at the big hotel there, and ten days ago I lost my letter of credit. I did not know what in the world to do. I was a stranger; I knew no one in Europe; I hadn't a penny in my pocket; I couldn't even send a telegram to London to get my lost letter replaced; my hotel bill was a week old, and the presentation of it imminent--so imminent that it could happen at any moment now. I was so frightened that my wits seemed to leave me. I tramped and tramped, back and forth, like a crazy person. If anybody approached me I hurried away, for no matter what a person looked like, I took him for the head waiter with the bill.

"I was at last in such a desperate state that I was ready to do any wild thing that promised even the shadow of help, and so this is the insane thing that I did. I saw a family lunching at a small table on the veranda, and recognized their nationality-- Americans--father, mother, and several young daughters-- young, tastefully dressed, and pretty--the rule with our people. I went straight there in my civilian costume, named my name, said I was a lieutenant in the army, and told my story and asked for help.

"What do you suppose the gentleman did? But you would not guess in twenty years. He took out a handful of gold coin and told me to help myself--freely. That is what he did."

The next morning the lieutenant told me his new letter of credit had arrived in the night, so we strolled to Cook's to draw money to pay back the benefactor with. We got it, and then went strolling through the great arcade. Presently he said, "Yonder they are; come and be introduced." I was introduced to the parents and the young ladies; then we separated, and I never saw him or them any m---

"Here we are at Farmington," said Twichell, interrupting.

We left the trolley-car and tramped through the mud a hundred yards or so to the school, talking about the time we and Warner walked out there years ago, and the pleasant time we had.

We had a visit with my niece in the parlor, then started for the trolley again. Outside the house we encountered a double rank of twenty or thirty of Miss Porter's young ladies arriving from a walk, and we stood aside, ostensibly to let them have room to file past, but really to look at them. Presently one of them stepped out of the rank and said:

"You don't know me, Mr. Twichell; but I know your daughter, and that gives me the privilege of shaking hands with you."

Then she put out her hand to me, and said:

"And I wish to shake hands with you too, Mr. Clemens. You don't remember me, but you were introduced to me in the arcade in Milan two years and a half ago by Lieutenant H."

What had put that story into my head after all that stretch of time? Was it just the proximity of that young girl, or was it merely an odd accident?

THE INVALID'S STORY

I seem sixty and married, but these effects are due to my condition and sufferings, for I am a bachelor, and only forty-one. It will be hard for you to believe that I, who am now but a shadow, was a hale, hearty man two short years ago, a man of iron, a very athlete!--yet such is the simple truth. But stranger still than this fact is the way in which I lost my health. I lost it through helping to take care of a box of guns on a two-hundred-mile railway journey one winter's night. It is the actual truth, and I will tell you about it.

I belong in Cleveland, Ohio. One winter's night, two years ago, I reached home just after dark, in a driving snow-storm, and the first thing I heard when I entered the house was that my dearest boyhood friend and schoolmate, John B. Hackett, had died the day before, and that his last utterance had been a desire that I would take his remains home to his poor old father and mother in Wisconsin. I was greatly shocked and grieved, but there was no time to waste in emotions; I must start at once. I took the card, marked "Deacon Levi Hackett, Bethlehem, Wisconsin," and hurried off through the whistling storm to the railway station. Arrived there I found the long white-pine box which had been described to me; I fastened the card to it with some tacks, saw it put safely aboard the express car, and then ran into the eating-room to provide myself with a sandwich and some cigars. When I returned, presently, there was my coffin-box back again, apparently, and a young fellow examining around it, with a card in his hands, and some tacks and a hammer! I was astonished and puzzled. He began to nail on his card, and I rushed out to the express car, in a good deal of a state of mind, to ask for an explanation. But no--there was my box, all right, in the express car; it hadn't been disturbed. [The fact is that without my suspecting it a prodigious mistake had been made. I was carrying off a box of guns which that young fellow had come to the station to ship to a rifle company in Peoria, Illinois, and he had got my corpse!] Just then the conductor sung out "All aboard," and I jumped into the express car and got a comfortable seat on a bale of buckets. The expressman was there, hard at work,--a plain man of fifty, with a simple, honest, good- natured face, and a breezy, practical heartiness in his general style. As the train moved off a stranger skipped into the car and set a package of peculiarly mature and capable Limburger cheese on one end of my coffin-box--I mean my box of guns. That is to say, I know now that it was Limburger cheese, but at that time I never had heard of the article in my life, and of course was wholly ignorant of its character. Well, we sped through the wild night, the bitter storm raged on, a cheerless misery stole over me, my heart went down, down, down! The old expressman made a brisk remark or two about the tempest and the arctic weather, slammed his sliding doors to, and bolted them, closed his window down tight, and then went bustling around, here and there and yonder, setting things to rights, and all the time contentedly humming "Sweet By and By," in a low tone, and flatting a good deal. Presently I began to detect a most evil and searching odor stealing about on the frozen air. This depressed my spirits still more, because of course I attributed it to my poor departed friend. There was something infinitely saddening about his calling himself to my remembrance in this dumb pathetic way, so it was hard to keep the tears back. Moreover, it distressed me on account of the old expressman, who, I was afraid, might notice it. However, he went humming tranquilly on, and gave no sign; and for this I was grateful. Grateful, yes, but still uneasy; and soon I began to feel more and more uneasy every minute, for every minute that went by that odor thickened up the more, and got to be more and more gamey and hard to stand. Presently, having got things arranged to his satisfaction, the expressman got some wood and made up a tremendous fire in his stove.

This distressed me more than I can tell, for I could not but feel that it was a mistake. I was sure that the effect would be deleterious upon my poor departed friend. Thompson--the expressman's name was Thompson, as I found out in the course of the night--now went poking around his car, stopping up whatever stray cracks he could find, remarking that it didn't make any difference what kind of a night it was outside, he calculated to make us comfortable, anyway. I said nothing, but I believed he was not choosing the right way. Meantime he was humming to himself just as before; and meantime, too, the stove was getting hotter and hotter, and the place closer and closer. I felt myself growing pale and qualmish, but grieved in silence and said nothing.

Soon I noticed that the "Sweet By and By" was gradually fading out; next it ceased altogether, and there was an ominous stillness. After a few moments Thompson said,

"Pfew! I reckon it ain't no cinnamon 't I've loaded up thish-yer stove with!"

He gasped once or twice, then moved toward the cof--gun-box, stood over that Limburger cheese part of a moment, then came back and sat down near me, looking a good deal impressed. After a contemplative pause, he said, indicating the box with a gesture,

"Friend of yourn?"

"Yes," I said with a sigh.

"He's pretty ripe, ain't he!"

Nothing further was said for perhaps a couple of minutes, each being busy with his own thoughts; then Thompson said, in a low, awed voice,

"Sometimes it's uncertain whether they're really gone or not,--seem gone, you know--body warm, joints limber--and so, although you think they're gone, you don't really know. I've had cases in my car. It's perfectly awful, becuz you don't know what minute they'll rise up and look at you!" Then, after a pause, and slightly lifting his elbow toward the box,-- "But he ain't in no trance! No, sir, I go bail for him!"

We sat some time, in meditative silence, listening to the wind and the roar of the train; then Thompson said, with a good deal of feeling,

"Well-a-well, we've all got to go, they ain't no getting around it. Man that is born of woman is of few days and far between, as Scriptur' says. Yes, you look at it any way you want to, it's awful solemn and cur'us: they ain't nobody can get around it; all's got to go--just everybody, as you may say. One day you're hearty and strong"--here he scrambled to his feet and broke a pane and stretched his nose out at it a moment or two, then sat down again while I struggled up and thrust my nose out at the same place, and this we kept on doing every now and then--" and next day he's cut down like the grass, and the places which knowed him then knows him no more forever, as Scriptur' says. Yes'ndeedy, it's awful solemn and cur'us; but we've all got to go, one time or another; they ain't no getting around it."

There was another long pause; then,--

"What did he die of?"

I said I didn't know.

"How long has he ben dead?"

It seemed judicious to enlarge the facts to fit the probabilities; so I said,

"Two or three days."

But it did no good; for Thompson received it with an injured look which plainly said, "Two or three years, you mean." Then he went right along, placidly ignoring my statement, and gave his views at considerable length upon the unwisdom of putting off burials too long. Then he lounged off toward the box, stood a moment, then came back on a sharp trot and visited the broken pane, observing,

"'Twould 'a' ben a dum sight better, all around, if they'd started him along last summer."

Thompson sat down and buried his face in his red silk handker-chief, and began to slowly sway and rock his body like one who is doing his best to endure the almost unendurable. By this time the fragrance--if you may call it fragrance--was just about suffocating, as near as you can come at it. Thompson's face was turning gray; I knew mine hadn't any color left in it. By and by Thompson rested his forehead in his left hand, with his elbow on his knee, and sort of waved his red handkerchief towards the box with his other hand, and said,--

"I've carried a many a one of 'em,--some of 'em considerable overdue, too,--but, lordy, he just lays over 'em all!--and does it easy Cap., they was heliotrope to HIM!"

This recognition of my poor friend gratified me, in spite of the sad circumstances, because it had so much the sound of a compliment.

Pretty soon it was plain that something had got to be done. I suggested cigars. Thompson thought it was a good idea. He said,

"Likely it'll modify him some."

We puffed gingerly along for a while, and tried hard to imagine that things were improved. But it wasn't any use. Before very long, and without any consultation, both cigars were quietly dropped from our nerveless fingers at the same moment. Thompson said, with a sigh,

"No, Cap., it don't modify him worth a cent. Fact is, it makes him worse, becuz it appears to stir up his ambition. What do you reckon we better do, now?"

I was not able to suggest anything; indeed, I had to be swallowing and swallowing, all the time, and did not like to trust myself to speak. Thompson fell to maundering, in a desultory and low-spirited way, about the miserable experiences of this night; and he got to referring to my poor friend by various titles,-- sometimes military ones, sometimes civil ones; and I noticed that as fast as my poor friend's effectiveness grew, Thompson promoted him accordingly,--gave him a bigger title. Finally he said,

"I've got an idea. Suppos' n we buckle down to it and give the Colonel a bit of a shove towards t'other end of the car? --about ten foot, say. He wouldn't have so much influence, then, don't you reckon?"

I said it was a good scheme. So we took in a good fresh breath at the broken pane, calculating to hold it till we got through; then we went there and bent over that deadly cheese and took a grip on the box. Thompson nodded "All ready," and then we threw ourselves forward with all our might; but Thompson slipped, and slumped down with his nose on the cheese, and his breath got loose. He gagged and gasped, and floundered up and made a break for the door, pawing the air and saying hoarsely, "Don't hender me! --gimme the road! I'm a-dying; gimme the road!" Out on the cold platform I sat down and held his head a while, and he revived. Presently he said,

"Do you reckon we started the Gen'rul any?"

I said no; we hadn't budged him.

"Well, then, that idea's up the flume. We got to think up something else. He's suited wher' he is, I reckon; and if that's the way he feels about it, and has made up his mind that he don't wish to be disturbed, you bet he's a-going to have his own way in the business. Yes, better leave him right wher' he is, long as he wants it so; becuz he holds all the trumps, don't you know, and so it stands to reason that the man that lays out to alter his plans for him is going to get left."

But we couldn't stay out there in that mad storm; we should have frozen to death. So we went in again and shut the door, and began to suffer once more and take turns at the break in the window. By and by, as we were starting away from a station where we had stopped a moment Thompson. pranced in cheerily, and exclaimed,

"We're all right, now! I reckon we've got the Commodore this time. I judge I've got the stuff here that'll take the tuck out of him."

It was carbolic acid. He had a carboy of it. He sprinkled it all around everywhere; in fact he drenched everything with it, rifle-box, cheese and all. Then we sat down, feeling pretty hopeful. But it wasn't for long. You see the two perfumes began to mix, and then--well, pretty soon we made a break for the door; and out there Thompson swabbed his face with his bandanna and said in a kind of disheartened way,

"It ain't no use. We can't buck agin him. He just utilizes everything we put up to modify him with, and gives it his own flavor and plays it back on us. Why, Cap., don't you know, it's as much as a hundred times worse in there now than it was when he first got a-going. I never did see one of 'em warm up to his work so, and take such a dumnation interest in it. No, Sir, I never did, as long as I've ben on the road; and I've carried a many a one of 'em, as I was telling you."

We went in again after we were frozen pretty stiff; but my, we couldn't stay in, now. So we just waltzed back and forth, freezing, and thawing, and stifling, by turns. In about an hour we stopped at another station; and as we left it Thompson came in with a bag, and said,--

"Cap., I'm a-going to chance him once more,--just this once; and if we don't fetch him this time, the thing for us to do, is to just throw up the sponge and withdraw from the canvass. That's the way I put it up." He had brought a lot of chicken feathers, and dried apples, and leaf tobacco, and rags, and old shoes, and sulphur, and asafoetida, and one thing or another; and he, piled them on a breadth of sheet iron in the middle of the floor, and set fire to them.

When they got well started, I couldn't see, myself, how even the corpse could stand it. All that went before was just simply poetry to that smell,--but mind you, the original smell stood up out of it just as sublime as ever,--fact is, these other smells just seemed to give it a better hold; and my, how rich it was! I didn't make these reflections there--there wasn't time--made them on the platform. And breaking for the platform, Thompson got suffocated and fell; and before I got him dragged out, which I did by the collar, I was mighty near gone myself. When we revived, Thompson said dejectedly,--

"We got to stay out here, Cap. We got to do it. They ain't no other way. The Governor wants to travel alone, and he's fixed so he can outvote us."

And presently he added,

"And don't you know, we're pisoned. It's our last trip, you can make up your mind to it. Typhoid fever is what's going to come of this. I feel it acoming right now. Yes, sir, we're elected, just as sure as you're born."

We were taken from the platform an hour later, frozen and insensible, at the next station, and I went straight off into a virulent fever, and never knew anything again for three weeks. I found out, then, that I had spent that awful night with a harmless box of rifles and a lot of innocent cheese; but the news was too late to save me; Imagination had done its work, and my health was permanently shattered; neither Bermuda nor any other land can ever bring it back tome. This is my last trip; I am on my way home to die.